Legends of Rock & Roll

The Grateful Dead

An unauthorized fan tribute

By: James Hoag

Paperback Edition

Other Paperbacks by James Hoag

Legends of Rock and Roll Series

Legends of Rock & Roll Volume 1 - The Fifties

Legends of Rock & Roll Volume 2 - The Sixties

Legends of Rock & Roll Volume 3 - The Seventies

The Beatles

Queen

Individual Beatles

John Lennon

Paul McCartney

George Harrison

Ringo Starr

Fifties

Everly Brothers

Sixties

Neil Diamond

Roy Orbison

The Beach Boys

Bob Dylan

The Doors

The Bee Gees

Seventies

Eagles

Bruce Springsteen

Eighties

Madonna

Legends of Country Music

Reba McEntire

Willie Nelson

Johnny Cash

George Jones

Merle Haggard

Garth Brooks

Waylon Jennings

(All Available at Amazon.com)

Table of Contents

Introduction   9

Before the Grateful Dead   11

Jerry Garcia   13

Phil Lesh   19

Bob Weir   22

Ron "Pigpen" McKernan   24

Bill Kreutzmann   26

Acid Tests   28

What's In a Name?   30

Summer of Love   32

Mickey Hart Joins the Band   35

"Anthem of the Sun"   37

"Aoxomoxoa"   39

First Truly Live Album   41

"Workingman's Dead"   45

"American Beauty"   47

A Classic Concert   49

Deadheads 51

Keith and Donna Godchaux Join the Band 53

The Death of Pigpen 55

The Wall of Sound 56

"Blues for Allah" 58

The Eighties 60

Jerry Goes Through a Rough Patch 62

"Touch of Gray" 63

The End of The Grateful Dead 66

After the Dead 68

Legacy of the Grateful Dead 72

Afterword 74

About the Author 76

Selected Discography 77

INTRODUCTION

"What a long, strange trip it's been."

"The Grateful Dead are trying to save the world." – Phil Lesh.

I was a fan of the Dead (I hope you won't mind if I just call them "the Dead," it's simpler that way), but I was never what you might call a "Deadhead." I did not travel around and try to attend every concert like some fans did. I do have a son-in-law, however, who did just that. He went so far as to have a recording of every different concert the Grateful Dead performed even if it wasn't available to the public.

Now, that's a true fan. How could anyone who lived in the late Sixties and early Seventies have not heard of the Grateful Dead? They were one of the greatest American bands of the time. I never actually got to see them perform, but I did hear a few of their albums and I was deep into MTV when the song "Touch of Grey" was released. I still like that song.

The Dead were the most important band of the psychedelic era (the last half of the Sixties) and, arguably, one of the most ground breaking bands in the history of Rock & Roll. They gradually increased their fans until hundreds of thousands would show up for a concert. The Grateful Dead are almost single handedly responsible for keeping the spirit of the Sixties alive through the next twenty years.

Anyone who has read any of the other *Legends of Rock & Roll* books knows what to expect here. I am not a biographer. I am a music lover. I grew up loving all kinds of music, and I love writing about it. You can't discuss the music without discussing the events surrounding the music. To know the music, you must know the people who wrote and played the music. For that, we have to delve into their lives and try to find out what makes them tick.

The Dead still perform, although now they are known by other names, and we'll get to that later. The keystone of the Grateful Dead was Jerry Garcia, as most everyone knows, and he died in 1995. When Jerry died, the Dead died with him. The other fellows have tried to keep the music alive without Jerry and for the most part, have done a great job of that. However, we all know that without Jerry, the Dead just aren't the Dead. Let's trace the history of the band and the people who made up the band and try to figure out what made it tick and become one of the great all time American bands.

BEFORE THE GRATEFUL DEAD

The Dead were formed in Palo Alto, California in 1965, but what happened before that? The founding members of the Dead were Jerry Garcia, who played guitar and contributed vocals; Bob Weir, also on guitar and vocals; Ron "Pigpen" McKernan, who played keyboards, harmonica and also contributed vocals; Phil Lesh, a bass player and, of course, vocals and last but not least, Bill Kreutzmann on drums.

As we shall see, the band began simple and slowly grew into what we know today as the Grateful Dead. Like many of the bands of the Sixties, they didn't just spring into existence fully formed but evolved into a great band.

Jerry Garcia first got together with Robert Hunter, another loner who was trying to make his way in the world. Both of them owned cars, but neither car worked, so somehow they parked them side by side in a vacant lot and lived together in their cars. They literally taught each other how to play the guitar and then they started getting gigs around Palo Alto, California where Jerry was living.

This was 1961, and the folk scene was where it was at. The hippie movement was in full swing, and folk music was in, so that's what they played. The first time they got paid for playing, they each made $5. They would hang out at the Tangent, which was a folk club in Palo Alto. They met Janis Joplin when she was just on her way up; just getting started. And they played when they could.

Soon Phil Lesh joined them and shortly after that Ron "Pigpen" McKernan started hanging around. Nothing was ever planned; it just happened. People got together who liked each other and thought they were compatible, and bands were born.

They played the clubs and the coffeehouses. They played bluegrass and folk and old-time country. They played anything the people wanted to hear. Dana Morgan's record store was a meeting place for the various musicians in Palo Alto. This is where Jerry met Bill Kreutzmann and where some friendships were formed. Bob Weir also joined the group. He was the youngest of the five and was still in high school when he officially joined the band.

The first group formed using members who would later become the Grateful Dead was Mother McCree's Uptown Jug Champions which was composed of three of the originals: Jerry, Pigpen, and Bob. It was, in a word, a jug band and Jerry said later that Bob Weir could play the jug better than anyone he had ever seen. An album of their music recorded back in 1964 was finally released in 1999 and a good deal of it can be found on YouTube, or you can still buy the album on Amazon. The music is primitive but is wonderful to listen to. It takes me back to the days I spent at the University of Michigan in the early Sixties.

Being a jug band was fun, but there wasn't much money in it. Pigpen declared that if they were to make any money, they needed to go "electric." They needed to "plug in." Therefore, in July of 1965, Mother McCree's became the Warlocks. Stay with me now because we are very close to the Grateful Dead. We first need to see how each of the original five got to the point where they are all playing together.

JERRY GARCIA

Jerome John "Jerry" Garcia was born on August 1, 1942 in Children's Hospital in San Francisco, California. His parents were Jose Ramon "Joe" Garcia and Ruth Marie "Bobbie" (née Clifford) Garcia. His father was Galician, which is a nationality that originated on the Iberian Peninsula. Today, it includes Spain, Portugal, Andorra, Gibraltar, and part of France. Dad's family immigrated to the United States in 1919. His mother is of Irish and Swedish ancestry and was born in San Francisco. They named him Jerome after the American composer, Jerome Kern who wrote many musicals in the Thirties and Forties.

Jerry had one older brother, Clifford Ramon, whom they called "Tiff." Tiff was about five years older than Jerry, being born in 1937. They grew up in what is called the Mission District of San Francisco.

To create a life of music, a person usually comes from some sort of musical background. Jerry's dad was a retired musician, having played in jazz bands throughout San Francisco. In fact, Jerry would later play in some of the same establishments his father played in years earlier. Dad, with a partner, had opened a bar in downtown San Francisco called The Four Hundred Club, so named because the address was 400 1st Street. Consequently, Jerry grew up around music. He took piano lessons off and on when he was young, but he never learned to read music. He just played by ear. His mother also played. Some of his fondest memories of his childhood are of the family around the piano, singing the songs of the day.

When Jerry was four, two things happened which changed his life. On vacation with the family in the Santa Cruz Mountains, he was holding the wood while his brother Clifford chopped firewood for the campfire. The axe accidently cut off 2/3 of his right middle finger.

They took his immediately to the hospital for treatment, but Jerry didn't even seem to notice that his finger was gone. He finally noticed it a few weeks later when the bandage came off. Jerry says he liked to show it to the other kids at school and freak them out.

Less than a year later, Jerry was standing on the bank of the Trinity River in Northwestern California and watched while his father lost his footing, fell into the river, and drowned. Several people have disputed whether Jerry actually saw his father die. Many say he was not even there, and there is no mention of him in the newspaper reports of the accident. However, Phil Lesh, one of the founders of the Grateful Dead, says he did see the accident and in an interview with *Rolling Stone* several years later, Jerry said, "I actually saw him go under." However, he was only four or five years old at the time, so who knows if he is remembering or if he's just creating images from the many times he has heard the story. I guess you will have to decide for yourself. Now there were just three of them: mom and the two boys. Mother Ruth decided to run the family business herself and so bought out dad's partner; thus, becoming the sole owner of the bar and nightclub he had been running.

Mom was now working fulltime and so she sent the boys to live with their grandparents, just a few blocks away. Jerry was an artistic boy and luckily, his teachers at the elementary school encouraged the talent. Over the next five years or so, he developed an interest in bluegrass and country music because his grandmother liked to listen to the Grand Ole Opry, all the way from Nashville, Tennessee. Jerry got his hands on a banjo and started practicing. This was his first stringed instrument, having played the piano for several years.

In 1953, his mother Ruth remarried. She married a fellow named Wally Matusiewicz and now with an entire family unit together they wanted to get out of the city, so they moved to Menlo Park, about 30 miles southeast of San Francisco. It was here that Jerry was introduced to rock and roll and rhythm and blues. The stars of 1953 were people like Ray Charles, John Lee Hooker, and B.B. King.

His brother, Clifford, was a little older and liked to sing along with the songs. He coerced Jerry into singing along with him, Jerry singing harmony.

You can't talk about the Grateful Dead or any member of the group without mentioning marijuana. Jerry was introduced to marijuana when he was fifteen years old. He had begun to smoke, and marijuana seemed like the next natural step. During an interview with *Rolling Stone Magazine* in 1972, Jerry told the interviewer, "Wow! Marijuana! Me and a friend of mine went up into the hills with two joints, the San Francisco foothills, and smoked these joints and just got so high and laughed and roared and went skipping down the streets doing funny things and just having a helluva time."

On his fifteenth birthday, his mother got him an accordion. She had noticed his interest in music and thought that it would make a good gift. Jerry was mortified. You didn't pick up girls playing an accordion. He pleaded with his mom to exchange the accordion for a guitar, and so she did. Jerry now had a used Danelectro guitar from a pawn shop, and he was on his way. His step-father Wally knew something about instruments and helped him get the guitar tuned and ready to play.

Jerry moved around a lot. The family moved back to San Francisco for a short time, but Jerry kept getting into trouble and so his mother thought he would do better in a small town again. This time they moved to Cazadero, California which is about 80 miles up the coast from San Francisco. Jerry was not happy. He had to spend 30 minutes on a bus each way to get to school each day and that made him even more unhappy.

One good thing did come out of Cazadero, though; he got together with some friends and started a band called The Chords. They won a local talent contest and got the opportunity to record a record. They did "Raunchy" (which was a big hit in 1957 by Bill Justis), but I don't know of any records that remain to this day.

High school just wasn't for Jerry. In 1960, when he was seventeen, he dropped out and proceeded to steal his mother's car. She turned him in, and his punishment was either jail or the Army. He choose the Army. He spent basic training at Fort Ord which was on Monterey Bay just south of San Jose, California. The base is closed now. After basic training, they sent him to the Presidio in San Francisco, but Jerry just couldn't stay out of trouble. He constantly missed role calls and was AWOL several times; consequently, his stay in the Army only lasted nine months. It's lucky he didn't get a dishonorable discharge. Instead, on December 4, 1960, the Army gave him a general discharge, and Jerry was free to do what he wanted.

The next few months are kind of a blur for Jerry. He bummed around and practiced his guitar and lived out of his car and, in general, didn't do much of anything. In February of 1961, he was involved in a car accident with some friends that killed one of them and broke Jerry's collarbone, among other scrapes and bruises. Jerry later said this accident acted as a kind of "wake-up call" for him. He decided he needed to get his life in order and make something of it.

He was interested in playing the guitar, and he loved art. He liked to paint and draw, but he realized that he couldn't both play guitar and draw, so he chose one. He decided to spend full time on the guitar and make something of his musical life.

In 1961, he met Robert Hunter who would become a collaborator with the Dead in later years. The two of them would play together at a local hangout, Kepler's Books, in Menlo Park. This store became a "beat" establishment for people who were into the bohemian lifestyle. The duo of Garcia/Hunter played there many times. Their first time, each earned $5 for the concert. Jerry was now a professional.

I was attending the University of Michigan in 1960, and the beat culture was alive and strong there. I remember very well getting together with friends who were "hippies." We would gather in someone's apartment and listen to this weird music and read poetry and smoke pot. I never participated in the pot smoking (not that I will ever admit), but I liked to listen to the music and the poetry. They were strange times.

Jerry met Phil Lesh in 1962. Phil became one of the founding members of the Dead and was their bass player. Phil later wrote in his autobiography that Jerry looked like the composer Claude Debussy. Do you know what Claude Debussy looks like? I certainly didn't and had to go online to find out. I guess I can see it, although it's a stretch.

To make ends meet, Jerry started taking in students to whom he would teach the banjo and the acoustic guitar. One such student was a boy named Bob Matthews who was still in high school. Matthews would later engineer several of the Grateful Dead albums. Matthews had a friend and asked Jerry if he would like to meet him. Therefore, on December 31, 1963, history was made as Jerry met Bob Weir.

In 1963, Jerry met his first wife, Sara Ruppenthal. They met one day while he was walking across the parking lot of a local mall, and she came riding by on a bicycle. He asked her if he could have a ride and so, riding on the back of the bicycle, holding his guitar, he and Sara got acquainted. She had been working at the Kepler Bookstore where Jerry played, so they might have seen each other before this. They were married on April 23, 1963 and in December they had their first and only child, a girl they named Heather. Jerry and Sara recorded and performed together for about a year.

Between 1962 and 1964, Jerry worked with several bands. He played bluegrass and folk music and became proficient on the guitar as well as the banjo and harmonica. Also, he contributed vocals. I love the names of the group from the mid-Sixties. One band he was with was the Sleepy Hollow Hog Stompers who consisted of Jerry, Marshall Leicester, and Dick Arnold. I was amazed to find a 49 minute concert by this group on YouTube dated June 11, 1962. It is clearly a live recording and not professional, but it can give you a feel for the type of music Jerry and his friends were playing in those days. Next, Jerry joined Mother McCree's Uptown Jug Champions, another bluegrass, old-time group who are also available on YouTube. It was while he was a member of Mother McCree's Uptown Jug Champions that he met number four of the original members of the Grateful Dead, Ron "Pigpen" McKernan, who also played for the band.

It was about this time that Jerry started experimenting with LSD. LSD was all the rage on the campuses and among the young in the Sixties. Asked if LSD brought him down or lifted him up, Jerry replied, "It freed me because I suddenly realized that my little attempt at having a straight life and doing that was really a fiction and just wasn't going to work out."

In 1965, Mother McCree's Uptown Jug Champions evolved into the Warlocks and added Phil Lesh and the final member of the group, Bill Kreutzmann on drums. The Warlocks didn't last long as they soon discovered that the name had already been taken by another band (a band who would someday become the Velvet Underground.)

All five were now in place for the creation of one the greatest American bands.

PHIL LESH

Phillip Chapman Lesh was born March 15, 1940 in Alta Bates Hospital in Berkley, California. He is the son of Frank and Barbara Chapman Lesh. Like Jerry Garcia's, Phil's father, Frank, was a musician, although Frank was more of an amateur musician. His dad also owned a small business and his mother worked outside the home as well. Phil was an only child and as he grew up, he was cared for and then ultimately given the responsibility of taking care of his maternal grandmother, Jewel Chapman.

Grandma liked to listen to classical music and so Phil was introduced to the greats of classical music as a young man. He remembers being truly moved listening to Braham's First Symphony. When he was eight years old, he started violin lessons. He joined the Young People's Symphony Orchestra in Berkley and continued to become more and more proficient in the orchestra. At age sixteen, he switched to trumpet and when he was in the 10th grade in high school, he transferred to Berkley High School so he could be a part of their music courses.

Unlike Jerry Garcia, who grew up being pretty much as a troublemaker, Phil Lesh graduated from high school and tried to enlist in the Army because he was afraid of being drafted. He failed the eye exam since he couldn't see anything without his glasses and was rejected. Elated that he didn't have to serve, he went to Junior College for a while and then transferred to the University of California Berkley.

It was while at Berkley that Phil heard Jerry Garcia play for the first time. Jerry was playing at a party Phil attended. Now, Phil was not a rock and roll type person. He had been brought up on Jazz and Classical and that's what he was studying in college. But after hearing

Jerry, Phil finally said, "I got it!" Jerry's music was, to quote Phil, "both spine-tingling and blood-curdling, presented without histrionics and with a fearless objectivity." This was the first time Phil could relate his classical work to the modern era, and he was hooked. Phil says he thought he had found a kindred spirit, but he was wrong; he had found a brother.

Phil had enrolled at Berkley as a music-major. However, he soon discovered that he was really beyond what they were teaching at the college level. He needed something more. He wanted to compose and U of C just wouldn't let him do that, so Phil and a friend, Tom Constanten, left and transferred to Mills College in Oakland, California. There, they enrolled in Luciano Berio's modernist music class. Berio was an Italian composer who is known for his work in experimental and electronic music. He died in 2003.

Working with Berio, Phil got the opportunity to compose. He also worked in engineering, recording, mixing, etc. Times were tough. Phil ended up working for the post office in order to make ends meet.

From 1960 until about 1963, Phil just sort of bummed around. He worked in California and in Las Vegas. The assassination of President Kennedy hit him really hard in November of 1963. He felt like screaming to the world, "What's the matter with you people?" Phil hit a new low that winter. He felt the world was spiraling out of control. He was twenty four years old, he didn't have a girlfriend, and he didn't have a real job. He had never finished college and so didn't have a degree or a career. He descended into depression and gloom. Then the answer came along. A friend came by one day and gave him 250 micrograms (or mike's) of LSD.

With his first use of LSD, Phil broke out of his depression and things began to happen for him. (Now, I'm not advocating the use of LSD; I'm only reporting what Phil says happened to him.) However, soon after his first "trip," he started getting work. He was asked to write a musical score for a San Francisco Mime Troupe. He wrote the musical accompaniment to the Mime movements.

1964 came and went and in 1965, Phil got fired from his job with the post office for refusing to cut his hair. He had seen the Beatles on screen and had seen how the girls reacted to them and so he combed his hair like the Beatles. The Postmaster was not amused and demanded he cut it. He could not represent the United States Government with hair like that, so Phil quit (or was fired; no one's sure except maybe Phil.)

In 1965, he and a girlfriend attended a party in Palo Alto where he once again ran into Jerry Garcia. The Warlocks were together by this time. Phil told Jerry he would like to learn the bass guitar, and Jerry encouraged him to do so. Bob Weir showed up at the party and brought the best weed Phil had ever had. They easily became acquainted. Bob was still in high school at the time.

BOB WEIR

Robert Hall Weir was born on October 16, 1947 in San Francisco, California. He was born to a single mother who gave him up for adoption shortly after his birth. I don't think anyone knows the name of his real mother, but his adoptive parents were Frederick and Eleanor Weir. Frederick was an Engineer, and Eleanor was a homemaker. Bob had one older brother, John, and a younger sister, Wendy.

Even though he was born in San Francisco, the Weirs took him to Atherton, California and that was where he was raised. Bob was a difficult student. He is proud of the fact that he was expelled from pre-school and almost every other school he attended as a boy. This was probably because he was dyslexic but also he was hard to get to know and had an irreverent attitude about everything. He attended several different schools as a boy but ended up at Fountain Valley School in Colorado Springs, Colorado.

Like the others, he was eventually kicked out of Fountain Valley and even though the website for the school lists him as an alumnus of the school, I'm not sure he ever actually graduated, but the important thing that happened there was he met a man who would be his lifelong friend, John Barlow. Barlow would work with Bob and the rest of the Grateful Dead for years.

One thing Bob was good at was athletics. He is the only one of the original five Grateful Dead that was an athlete. He played track and football and was good at both. His parents wanted him to play an instrument but since he really didn't get along too well with others, it needed to be an instrument that a person could play by himself. He tried the piano but didn't do too well with that. He tried the trumpet (just like Phil Lesh), but that didn't work either. Then someone thought of the guitar, and they struck gold. This was it. This was what he was meant to play.

Bob says his curriculum in high school was guitars and girls. After being kicked out of yet another school, Weir went to California. He was sixteen at the time, a minor, and was taking charge of his own life. I wonder what his parents thought of this and why they let him go.

He was bumming around the streets of Palo Alto when he heard banjo music coming from a local record shop called Dana's Music. Inside the store, Jerry Garcia was playing and the two became close friends. Bob first became Jerry's student and then, when Jerry was absent, Bob became the teacher. He would spend his evenings at a local nightclub called the Tangent where he saw Janis Joplin and Jefferson Airplane play. And, of course, Jerry Garcia played there.

A year later, Jerry and Ron "Pigpen" McKernan were forming a band called Mother McCree's Uptown Jug Champions. It would be a blues and a rock and roll band. They asked Bob to be the rhythm guitarist. Bob was the youngest member of the group.

RON "PIGPEN" MCKERNAN

Ronald Charles McKernan was born September 8, 1945 in San Bruno, California, which is a suburb of San Francisco. Finding out information about his parents has proven to be a daunting task. It appears that his father was Phil McKernan who was a radio disk jockey on station KRE-AM radio station transmitting out of Berkeley, California. He specialized in playing rhythm and blues music and was known on the air as "Cool Breeze." Phil was also a boogie-woogie piano player in his spare time. Ron's mother was Esther McKernan. Ron is buried in Palo Alto next to a couple named Frank and Alice McKernan; these are believed to be his grandparents.

Ron grew up, like the others, listening to music. He especially liked the black music of the Fifties. I'm sure his father contributed to that taste in music. He was the epitome of the rebel teenager. It is said that he had a biker image, but I'm pretty sure he didn't have a bike. He taught himself to play the piano, but he didn't like school. There came a time when the principal of his high school agreed with Ron that school just wasn't working for him and so Ron quit.

Ron met Jerry Garcia when he was only about fourteen. Jerry would come over to the house and they would sit in Ron's room and play music. Ron wanted to learn the blues guitar, and Jerry was a teacher, so Ron learned to play from Jerry. I've heard that when Jerry would come over, he would be amazed at how messed up Ron's room was. Jerry called it a ghetto. Stuff was everywhere. Ron would hang around in just a tee-shirt and underpants. He didn't care. His mother actually came to his room every few hours or so and check to see if he was still alive. The place looked like a "pigpen" and, I suspect, that's where he got the nickname.

I might be wrong about that, however. I read two other versions of how he got the nickname. One said that a friend of his from high school named him "Pigpen" because of his "funky" approach to life. Then again, in an essay written for a box set of Grateful Dead material called *The Golden Road (1965-1973),* it states that a girlfriend gave him the nickname because she thought he looked like the dirty character from the comic strip "Peanuts." Therefore, it's anyone's guess as to how he got the name.

The fact remains that everyone called Ron "Pigpen" or usually just Pig for short. Since he knew Jerry, he began to hang around the coffeehouses where Jerry played. One day, Jerry invited him on stage to play with the group. Ron would play the harmonica and sing along, and Jerry was impressed. Once Ron had an "in" with Jerry, he was a member of the group for life.

BILL KREUTZMANN

William Kreutzmann (pronounced Kroytz-mahn) was born May 7, 1946 in Palo Alto, California. His father was Bill senior, but I have been unable to find his mother's name. His mother was a teacher of dance at Stanford University.

Bill took to the drums at an early age, actually starting to play them when he was in sixth grade (at about the age of twelve). It was 1957. Like most boys that age, he joined the school band as a drummer, but he didn't last long. His teacher told him he couldn't keep a beat and kicked him out of the band, but his parents still believed in him and encouraged him to keep practicing and playing as much as he could. He would play for the routines his mother choreographed at Stanford.

He started taking private lessons from a graduate student, Lee Anderson, who worked as a jazz drummer in his spare time. Anderson lived right near the author Ken Kesey (who we will talk about later) and had a profound effect on Bill. During High School, Bill formed two different bands with fellow students: The Wildwood Boys and Legends. Legends was an R&B band that performed in uniforms and played primarily for YMCA dances.

He first saw Jerry Garcia play one night when he and some friends visited the Tangent, a folk club in Palo Alto. It was just Jerry, Pigpen, and Hunter, but it was a start, and Bill was enthralled.

While still in high school, Bill got a job working at Dana Morgan's music store in Palo Alto. His father had an old banjo he wanted to sell, so he took it down to Morgan's and sold it to a guy that just happened to walk in the store that day. (Actually, it wasn't that much of a coincidence since Jerry worked at the store.) This was the first time Bill had had a chance to meet Jerry, and the two became almost instant friends.

At sixteen, his parents got divorced, and his mother sent him to a prep school in Prescott, Arizona. He tried out for football and was quickly kicked off the team. Somehow, his dad knew he needed something else and so sent him his drums in large wooden crates. Bill actually met the author Aldous Huxley while he was at the school. Bill said he didn't know who Huxley was but that he had a profound impact on him.

Huxley wrote two books that were to have a great influence on American culture, even though Huxley, himself, was British. "Brave New World" was written in 1931 and "The Doors of Perception" was written in 1954. The latter book became the bible of the drug culture in the late Sixties and is the origin of the name of the rock group "The Doors."

In 1963, Bill got a chance to play with the guys when he was invited to join The Zodiacs, the band Jerry Garcia put together when Hunter left the band. Bill sometimes had to use a fake-ID to get into bars where they played since he was underage, being only nineteen at the time. He played under the name of Bill Summers. The Zodiacs morphed into the Warlocks in 1965 and then as we've seen before, the Warlocks became the Grateful Dead, and Bill was along for almost the entire ride.

ACID TESTS

You may have heard of Ken Kesey. He wrote the best seller *One Flew over the Cuckoo's Nest* in 1962. If you have not read the book, you should. The movie with Jack Nicholson is good, but the book is much better. Kesey considered himself a link between the Beat Generation of the Fifties and the Hippies of the Sixties.

Kesey lived in Palo Alto, and Jerry and the crew got to know him pretty well. In fact, the Warlocks became the house band for parties that Kesey would throw at his house. He called them "Acid Tests." Now, in 1963, LSD was still legal and the college students were tripping out all of the time. Kesey would hold these parties and hand out LSD (and other psychoactive drugs) to the people (known as the Merry Pranksters) who came to the parties. This became quite well known around San Francisco, and Kesey's parties became legendary.

Since the drug was legal, Kesey actually advertised around San Francisco for people to come to the parties. The posters read "CAN YOU PASS THE ACID TEST?" This led to a book which was very popular during the mid-Sixties by Tom Wolfe called *The Electric Kool-Aid Acid Test*. The boys in the band got an invite to the first party Kesey threw and then they started coming every week and became regulars. At first, they just came to party and get high; no one thought about music but then someone said that music would strengthen the experience and so the guys started bringing their instruments and became the house band. They were first known as the Warlocks. Everybody got a "drug" name; for instance, they called Jerry "Captain Trips," and Phil was "Reddy Kilowatt," Bill was just known as "Bill the Drummer," which seems rather lame to me, and of course Pigpen already had a nickname so they just called him Pigpen. Not much originality among the drug crowd, I guess.

This all lasted about six months; a time during which the guys and the Pranksters who followed them were seldom not high. Kesey was busted, finally, for distributing the drugs. I'm not sure if they were finally made illegal or if the authorities were just tired of the foolishness. To keep from going to jail, Kesey fled to Mexico.

The Warlocks were along for the ride until someone noticed that the name Warlocks was already taken by another band. You can't register a band name if someone else already has the rights to the name, so a change had to be made.

WHAT'S IN A NAME?

Since another band had already taken the name, they needed a new one. This is the story that Phil Lesh tells: "The group was sitting around Phil's apartment one day talking about it and suggesting names. Many really silly names were proposed until finally Jerry opened a Funk & Wagnall's Folklore Dictionary and blindly stabbed his finger down on a page. His finger landed on 'grateful dead.'" At first, the guys didn't really like the name. It was a little depressing. Here is the story of what the name actually means.

When a person dies leaving a debt, sometimes the body is not properly buried, but is actually just placed along the side of a road. A traveler may come along and see the body and decide to pay whatever debt the deceased person had so that he could have a decent burial. The dead person now becomes a grateful dead. The traveler then goes on his way and comes across the spirit of the dead person in the form of an animal, who then helps the traveler with some problem he might have.

The guys then found out that a man by the name of Francis Childs, an American scholar in the late 1800's, was a folklorist or a person who studies folklore. Childs classified ballads and one of the types of ballads he classified were called grateful dead ballads. After the guys heard that, they decided to go with the name. The first time the band played after changing their name was at one of Kesey's Acid Test parties on December 4, 1965, but that event was not recorded. There are rumored to be bootleg tapes of the show, but I can't be sure. The first time they played in public after selecting the name which was recorded was with Bill Graham at the Fillmore in San Francisco on January 8, 1966. Graham hated the name and during the show, his people would put up placards at the side of the stage announcing who was playing. For the Dead, the sign read, "The Grateful Dead formerly

The Warlocks." Graham did come around eventually and came to see how perfect the name was for the group.

You've heard of the Haight-Ashbury District of San Francisco. That was where it was happening in the Sixties. The entire group, along with a couple friends and girlfriends for each of the guys, all lived together in one house (you might say communally) at 710 Ashbury Street which is just around the corner from Haight Street. The area still exists to this day, although I don't think it's as bohemian as it was then. You would walk out the front door of your house and instantly you were assaulted with color and sound. The culture of love was alive and well in San Francisco. Everyone loved everyone else, and everyone was friendly with everyone else. The streets were alive with the color of flowers and costumes that people wore. There was magic in the air.

The story of the Grateful Dead would not be complete without a mention of Owsley Stanley, known in San Francisco as the "Acid King." Owsley was the man behind the "Acid Tests" that Ken Kesey held. He was the supplier. He was the first private citizen to produce LSD on a large scale. This was when it was legal. His big problem was he continued to manufacture it even after it was declared illegal. Between 1965 and 1967, Owsley manufactured more than 1.25 million doses of LSD. He worked as a sound engineer for the band for a while, and he was the person that arranged for the band to live at 710 Ashbury Street for several years.

SUMMER OF LOVE

1967 would become known as the year of the Summer of Love in San Francisco. A precursor to that was a concert which was held at Golden Gate Park on January 14. It was known as "A Gathering of Tribes for a Human Be-In" or as most people called it, just "The Human Be-In" and was almost single handedly responsible for putting Haight-Ashbury on the International map. The main reason for the event was that California had made LSD illegal and the counterculture that was Haight-Ashbury and a lot of San Francisco wanted the world to know that the drug was a good thing. It increased consciousness and liberated thinking.

The Human Be-In was kind of an early Woodstock with mostly local bands playing and this included the Grateful Dead. Others bands playing were Jefferson Airplane, Quicksilver Messenger Service, and Big Brother and Holding Company. Allen Ginsberg was there to read poetry. The guru of LSD, Timothy Leary, was there. Phil describes the occasion as a "river of color." The stage was two flat-bed trucks strapped together. The event was kicked off by a Buddhist chant led by Ginsberg. Then the bands played, the people danced, and everyone had a great time. The summer of love had officially begun.

The Dead did "Dancing in the Street" which was a Dead version of the Martha & the Vandellas song from 1964. You can find a 13 minute version of the song on YouTube. They performed "Morning Dew," "Good Morning Little Schoolgirl," several others, and then closed with their standard closing song "Viola Lee Blues." They heard later that the famous jazz trumpeter, Dizzy Gillespie, was in the audience and remarked to a friend "Who are those guys? They sure can swing."

The next major appearance by the band was on January 29, 1967 when they played at the Mantra-Rock Dance held at the Avalon Ballroom in San Francisco. It was held as a promotional vehicle for the followers of International Society for Krishna Consciousness. Many up-and-coming bands played for the event including Big Brother and the Holding Company (featuring Janis Joplin) and a new band that was almost completely unknown at the time, Moby Grape. And, of course, the Dead were there.

The guys had been trying for a record deal for months and shortly after the Mantra-Rock Dance, they got word that they should come to Los Angeles to record their first album which would be called *The Grateful Dead*. They made the trip and signed with Warner Brothers Records and proceeded to start work on the album. They thought they had gotten a pretty good contract. They were given artistic control over what they recorded, so the company didn't have the power to change their sound. However, they overlooked one thing: the record company owned the work, forever. This would prove to be a problem later on.

They picked David Hassinger to produce the album because of the work he had done previously. He had worked with the Rolling Stones "(I Can't Get No) Satisfaction" and with the Jefferson Airplane on *Surrealistic Pillow*, great music from the Sixties. Jerry Garcia actually played on the Jefferson Airplane album and had suggested its title to the group.

The Dead were used to playing live in front of an audience. Recording in a studio was something new and they had a hard time adjusting to the environment; songs that they did live, they could go on and on and they could play as long as they wanted to, but albums have limits and so many songs had to be shortened to fit. According to Phil, the only song which approximated how they play in person was "Viola Lee Blues" which timed out at a hair over ten minutes on the original version of the album.

If you check out an image of the album online, you'll see some unreadable words across the top of the front cover. They originally said "In the land of the dark, the ship of the sun is driven by the Grateful Dead" which, according to legend, is from the Egyptian "Book of the Dead." However, before the album was printed, the band requested that everything except their name be distorted so as to be unreadable.

Another distinction this album has is it contains the song "Cream Puff War" which is one of only two Jerry Garcia lyrics that have ever been recorded (works that only he wrote, not a collaboration.) The album was released as just the self-titled *The Grateful Dead*. Phil says it should have been called *San Francisco's Grateful Dead*. 1967 was a little early for FM radio which is where an album like this would be played. AM stations in the San Francisco area played some cuts from the album, but it wasn't really heard that much outside of the bay area. In 2011, the album was released on vinyl recorded from the original 1967 masters. This was the first time in forty years that the album was released in this form.

MICKEY HART JOINS THE BAND

In late 1967, there was a singular event at the Fillmore in Los Angeles which would ultimately affect the band greatly. Bill Graham booked both Chuck Berry and Count Basie at the club at the same time. Count Basie had a drummer named Sonny Payne and one night, a guy showed up to watch the show. This was Mickey Hart, who was himself a drummer. He was born in Brooklyn, New York on September 11, 1943 and had played the drums for the Air Force Band. He came to the Fillmore to see Sonny Payne play.

Mickey grew up without a father. Lenny Hart, his father, had left the family before he was born. While stationed in California, Mickey happened to meet up with Lenny and a relationship, of sorts, developed. After being discharged from the Air Force, Mickey went home to New York to continue his music career. Soon, he received a letter from Lenny asking him to work with him in a drum store he owned in San Francisco, so this puts Mickey in the San Francisco area and sets up the situation where he can meet the members of the Grateful Dead.

In the crowd at the Fillmore were also members of the Grateful Dead, at least Phil Lesh and Bill Kreutzmann were there. A total stranger came up to Mickey Hart and, pointing to Bill, said, "See that guy over there? Bill Kreutzmann, he's the drummer for the Grateful Dead. You should meet him." So the stranger introduces Mickey to Bill and then disappears into the crowd never to be seen again.

But the deed was done. Mickey recognized in Bill a kindred spirit, and they were to become close friends. A few nights later, the Dead were playing at a local club when Mickey was in the audience. During a break, Bill came out and found Mickey, procured another set of drums somewhere, and had Mickey join the band. This was the first time Mickey played with the band, and he soon became a regular member.

Believe it or not, the Grateful Dead is the first band ever to have two drummers. They found that they could play off of each other and create sounds like no one else. No other band had ever done this and, I think, this is one reason that the Dead were so loved by their fans.

Mickey Hart and Bill Kreutzmann became known as the "Rhythm Devils" and in later concerts almost always gave an extended drum solo during one of the songs. (Or maybe you'd call it a duo.)

"ANTHEM OF THE SUN"

Consequently, now there were six members in the band. They also brought in guest players who weren't really Grateful Dead members like Tom Constanten who was an old friend of Phil's. They started work on their second album *Anthem of the Sun*. Having not been totally happy with the way the first album turned out, they wanted this one to be right. They were, after all, a live band, and they wanted this to come across in their recordings. This was a difficult task and after a month of work, the album was only half done.

Their producer was getting tired of all the shenanigans that the band went through to produce their music. Tom Constanten played the piano and to get the sounds they wanted, he used what is called a prepared piano. Now he wasn't the first to do this, but he certainly came up with some unique ways of doing it. Preparing a piano involves putting foreign objects on the sound board to alter the sound that the strings make when the hammer strikes them. At one point, he used a common child's spinning top which would spin around in the sound board and produce completely random sounds. There was no way to predict exactly what sound would come out. The guys loved it.

However, their producer, David Hassinger, didn't like it so much. He was tired of it all and just wanted to get the album done. One day, Bob Weir came into the studio (they were recording in New York at the time) and declared that he wanted to produce the sound of "thick air." Hassinger blew up and shouted that there isn't any such thing as "thick air" and on the spot, he quit. I think I can understand how he felt. I'm not sure the guys really knew what they were looking for. It was mostly a case of trying something and if it sounds good, then use it. If not, then try something else.

They got a new producer, Dan Healy, who had been their sound engineer and eventually finished the album. The album had been started in November of 1967 and wasn't released until July of 1968. It only has five songs on it, which is more in line with the live feel that they were trying to reproduce. In fact, a lot of the music is actually taken from live concerts and the music is blended in with the studio work. The longest song "Alligator" is over eleven minutes long. This was unheard of in the days of AM radio and before the days of FM when you might hear a ten minute song or longer. These songs certainly wouldn't work as singles, but the guys were happy with the result.

"AOXOMOXOA"

Their next studio album was uniquely named *Aoxomoxoa* (pronounced "ox-oh-mox-oh-ah".) It was originally titled *Earthquake Country*. The album has a strange cover. It was designed by Rick Griffin who was famous for his psychedelic posters which were seen all over San Francisco. The band hired him to do the cover and said just give us something. They gave him full freedom to design whatever he wanted.

You may have noticed that the word "Aoxomoxoa" is a palindrome (reads the same forward and backwards.) If you examine the cover that Griffin designed, the words "Grateful Dead" which are drawn in a wild psychedelic pattern are an ambigram which can be read as "we ate the acid." An ambigram is another way of looking at a design. The theory is if you cover the lower 2/3 of the words "Grateful Dead" you will see the words "we ate the acid." I tried it, looked at it every which way I could, and I couldn't see it, but maybe you can. So what does *Aoxomoxoa* mean? According to Rick Griffin's wife, it is a surfer's paradise of sunshine, blue sky, and life.

The Grateful Dead just about had this album done when Ampex, a manufacturer of recording equipment, came out with the first 16-track tape recorder. The album so far had been recorded on 8-track. Well, the guys couldn't have that, so they essentially started all over again and re-recorded the album on 16-track. This took some time as they had to acquaint themselves with the equipment. Needless to say, the record company was not happy. There are other firsts associated with this album beside the 16-track machine. It is the first album that Tom Constanten plays on as a regular member of the Dead. Now there were seven regular members. This was also their first album to be completely recorded in or near San Francisco. When David Hassinger left as producer, they were no longer constrained to recording on the east coast, so they returned home to do their work.

And, it was the first album to use Jerry Garcia's old friend Robert Hunter as a lyricist. He came on full time for the band and Hunter and Jerry became a great writing team, sort of like Lennon/McCartney. There were acoustic songs on this album, also. "Mountains of the Moon" and "Dupree's Diamond Blues" were done acoustically and this was the first time Phil Lesh played an acoustic bass guitar on a recording.

Fans of the Grateful Dead consider *Aoxomoxoa* to be part of the band's "experimental" period, and this album represents the best of that period.

FIRST TRULY LIVE ALBUM

Using their new "toy," the 16-track recorder, they proceeded to take it with them everywhere they went and recorded the band live in various places. The album, called *Live/Dead,* was recorded mainly at the Avalon Ballroom and the Fillmore West (which was called the Carousel in 1968.) "Dark Star" and "St. Stephen" were taken from the February 27, 1969 show at the Carousel. "The Eleven" and "Turn on Your Love Light" were from the January 26, 1969 show at the Avalon Ballroom. "Death Don't Have No Mercy," "Feedback," and "And We Bid You Goodnight" were from the March 2, 1969 show at the Carousel.

The album was released on November 10, 1969, and it peaked at number 64 on the Billboard Album charts. That was as high as they had gotten up to this point. *Rolling Stone Magazine* has since declared that *Live/Dead* is number 244 on their list of the *500 Greatest Albums of All Time.*

The band had a big problem, though. I was not aware that when a band records an album or any other type of recording, they are responsible for the costs of doing the recording. Normally, the record company gives the band an advance on royalties to pay for the recording but if the record doesn't sell, then who pays off that debt? The Dead's recording sessions were very expensive since they sometimes did a song dozens of times before they got what they wanted. When they switched from 8-Track to 16-track, they essentially threw out weeks of work and all of that needed to be paid for. To make matters worse, the albums weren't selling that well, so far. Consequently, the band was deep in debt to Warner Brothers Records.

The live album did do better than the previous studio albums and just about got them out of the hole. It sold better and had been cheaper to make, so the profit was better. They were able to pay off some of their debt. They needed a new manager and so they hired Mickey Hart's Dad, Lenny Hart, who had owned a drum store with Mickey and now worked as an Evangelical Preacher. Lenny did an OK job but not great. He tried to convince the guys to star in a movie, something they didn't want to do at all.

One of the worse things he did was to negotiate the renewal of their contract with Warner Brothers Records without their knowledge. Now, the problem wasn't that they didn't want to renew, they just would have liked to have been kept in the loop, and Lenny was excluding them. They even received a signing bonus that they never knew about until later because the bonus went right toward their debt, and they didn't see a penny of it.

In August of 1969, the band travelled to upstate New York to attend "Three Days of Peace & Music;" in other words, Woodstock. The Merry Pranksters were there and greeted the guys warmly. The band played on late Saturday night, which was day number two of the festival. They played a lineup of music that was heard at most Grateful Dead concerts. They started with "St Stephen," followed that with "Mama Tried" (a Merle Haggard song), then "Dark Star," "High Time," and ending with "Turn on Your Love Light." I'm not sure if there would have been more music, but the stage amps overloaded during the playing of "Turn on Your Love Light" and fuses blew out and the set came to a close.

The band started playing at 10:30 p.m., so it was dark while they were playing. Their set ended at 12:05 a.m. when the power went out. A storm had blown in on the area and there was rain and lightning. Just plugging in the instruments was taking your life in your hands, but they persevered. The ground became a sea of mud and people were dancing, covered with mud. If you've seen the concert movie, you know what I mean. The stage actually started to slide forward on the mud, and they were afraid it would reach the audience. The boys finished their set with "Love Light" and quietly left the area.

The next big event for the band was a concert in the bay area which was promoted by the Rolling Stones. They were coming to town and needed a venue to play in. They could expect at least a hundred thousand people and so needed a big place. The date of the concert was December 6, 1969. The promoters tried to get Golden Gate Park for the concert but were refused, so they finally settled on Altamont Raceway. They made one big mistake, however. They hired the Hell's Angels motorcycle club (or asked, nobody hires the Angels to do anything) to protect the generators from the crowd, but the Angels interpreted that to mean they were in charge of security.

When the band arrived at Altamont, the front of the stage was lined with motorcycles and the Angels were not allowing anyone near it. Unfortunately, this included the band members. Marty Balin of Jefferson Airplane had been assaulted when he tried to stop an Angel from beating up one of the spectators. When the Dead attempted to go on stage to check their equipment, the Angels stopped them and sent them back to their trailers. The Rolling Stones did perform and so did other bands, but when the band got word that a man had been stabbed in the audience, they said this is not for us and they left. Therefore, even though they were on the bill to play the concert, they never actually did play.

They later said that Woodstock and Altamont were two sides of the same coin. Woodstock was love and peace and drugs. Everyone was high and happy and there wasn't one incident of violence even though there were 400, 000 people there. Altamont had close to a riot and someone actually got stabbed (not sure if he lived or not) and was the exact opposite of Woodstock.

Lenny Hart, father of Mickey, was acting as their manager through all of this and weird things began to happen. Lenny wouldn't let the guys look at the books. He told them they wouldn't understand them, anyway. Pig's organ was repossessed right while they were on stage at a concert. Checks that they received for various things started disappearing. Growing suspicious of Lenny, they decided to confront him and demanded to see the books. Lenny, however, got wind of what was happening and, taking his girlfriend, escaped to Mexico.

I've seen figures that Lenny stole about $75,000 before they became aware of what he was doing. The one that was hurt the most was Mickey, who felt deeply sorry that his father had stolen from the band. Someone suggested they send the Hells Angels down to Mexico to bring Lenny back, but that was never done. Jerry said no, Karma will catch up with him; we don't need to get violent. Sure enough, two years later, Lenny was caught and sentenced to serve time for his deed and the band was able to recover about a third of the money that was taken.

But Mickey never got over it. The moral here is to never hire your relatives to help you run your business. The group hired a new manager and accountants; professionals who knew what they were doing and put the band back on a solid financial footing.

"WORKINGMAN'S DEAD"

Work was started on their next album, *Workingman's Dead*. This album took just nine days to record. They had learned their lesson on paying for recording time. They realized they couldn't afford to keep tying up the studio for weeks on end looking for perfection in their recordings. The name of the album comes from a comment Jerry made to his friend Robert Hunter. He said to him, "this album is turning into a workingman's dead version of the band." The album was released in June of 1970.

Things were not good for the band at this time. They were dealing with the incident with Lenny Hart and his stealing so much money from them. They had just come back from New Orleans where they were busted for drug possession. They're lucky they didn't serve jail time for that. And the expenses of *Aoxomoxoa* were weighing heavily on them. Jerry told the band, "Let's just get it the hell out of the way." They just wanted the album over.

Even with all the problems and negative vibes, the album still turned out to be a Grateful Dead classic. It charted at number twenty seven on the Billboard Pop Album chart which was higher than any previous album. *Rolling Stone Magazine* later ranked the album at number 262 on their list of the *500 Greatest Albums of All Time*.

Jerry says they were trying to copy the style of Crosby, Stills, and Nash. They loved the harmonies of C, S, & N and wanted the album to sound like that. I think they succeeded. Go listen to "Uncle John's Band" on YouTube which is from the album. Stephen Stills had said that the voice could be an instrument, and the Dead took that to heart and used their voices in a way that they had never done before.

There are a number of theories as to who Uncle John is. Some say that he is Mississippi John Hurt, a country blues singer from, where else,

Mississippi, who was an influence on the band. Others say he could be John the Baptist from the Bible. In the biography "Dark Star" by Robert Greenfield, he says it refers to Jerry Garcia, himself, whose middle name is John. Warner Brothers Records released it as a single, but it only reached number 69 on the charts. It did get a lot of radio airplay, however.

"AMERICAN BEAUTY"

The next album, *American Beauty,* which was released in November 1, 1970, was a lot like *Workingman's Dead* and is also considered one of their best albums. It is ranked by *Rolling Stone Magazine* as number 258 of the *500 Greatest Albums of All Time.* Robert Hunter is listed as the writer or co-writer of almost every song on the album.

A highlight of the album has to be "Truckin,'" which became something of a signature song for the Dead. (Actually, the real signature song of the band was "Dark Star" which they played at almost every concert and never the same way twice.) According to the United States Library of Congress, in 1997, the song was declared a national treasure. Now, how many rock bands can say that they recorded a national treasure? The song was shorted a bit so it could be released as a single and peaked at number 64 on the Hot 100. This would be the highest the band reached on the pop singles charts until seventeen years later when they hit the Top 10 with their only Top 40 single, "Touch of Grey." The song is noteworthy because of its rhythm which the band calls "shuffling" and the words which all have an alternate meaning. I don't pretend to understand all of it, but I did recognize the line "Houston, too close to New Orleans" which I'm sure refers to the time the band was busted in New Orleans for drug possession. Later in the song, they say, "Busted, down on Bourbon Street," which I'm sure refers to the same incident. The most famous line in the song is "what a long, strange trip it's been" which was actually used as a title of a Greatest Hits album later in the Seventies.

"Truckin'" seems to be the perfect Grateful Dead song. It includes everything there is to know about the band. All of the cities are mentioned: Chicago, New York, Detroit, Houston; the drugs, "livin' on reds, vitamin C, and cocaine". I already talked about being busted in New Orleans.

The first song Phil Lesh sang solo was also from the *American Beauty* album. "Box of Rain" became a favorite of the fans and people would yell out, "Let Phil sing." The song is a tribute to his father who had died in September of 1970. That fall of 1970 saw the death of several people who were important to the guys of the Grateful Dead. Phil's father died in early September of 1970. That was followed by the death of Jimi Hendrix in London on September 18. No one is sure how Hendrix died, but the autopsy said that he had died by strangling on his own vomit as a result of taking barbiturates.

Ten days later, Jerry's mother, Bobbie, passed away. She had been involved in a pretty bad automobile accident in August and she never recovered from that. Then, on October 4, 1970, Janis Joplin died of a heroin overdose. That's four deaths in a little over a month; all people who were close or related to the band members. I'm not sure how they could complete an album through all of that, but they did. "Box of Rain" became a tribute song to anyone who had lost a loved one.

American Beauty became one of their best-loved albums and of the ten songs on the album eight of them remained as part of their live shows for as long as the band existed.

A CLASSIC CONCERT

I have to tell the story of what is probably the most classic Dead concert of them all. I guess that's a matter of opinion, but it sure impressed me. I have Phil Lesh's autobiography *Searching for the Sound – My Life with the Grateful Dead* to thank for this story.

In February of 1970, the band travelled to New York to play the Fillmore East on East 6th Street in the East Village. The club was only open for a little over three years, but oh, how I wish I had lived in New York City during that time. The Fillmore East was host to acts that a poor country boy like me can only dream about.

The nights that the Dead played there, they shared the stage with a group called "Love," who were also from California. Opening for them both was a brand new band that was just getting started, The Allman Brothers band. It turned out that members of Fleetwood Mac were in the building just to watch the show, so the Dead launch into their set and during "Dark Star," Duane Allman calmly comes on stage, plugs in, and starts playing along, so the band adjusts to the newcomer. Next to appear on stage is Peter Green of Fleetwood Mac, and he starts playing. All of this is impromptu. Gregg Allman comes on stage and sits down at the organ and joins in. Then Butch Trucks of Fleetwood starts playing the drums.

Everyone is changing the arrangement on the fly as these new people join the group and before anyone realizes it, there are five guitarist, four drummers, an organist, and over everything, you can hear Pigpen roaring away. You would think it would be just a cacophony of sound but no, it was surprisingly coherent and everyone had the time of their lives. Can you even imagine being in the audience for a performance like this and listening to history take place right in front of your eyes? This went on all night and when the band finally said good night to the audience and filed outside to load their gear, they realized that the sun was coming up.

Phil Lesh says, "*This* is what it's all about."

In 1970, the band played 142 shows on the road, the second largest number in the history of the band, both before and since. This was a busy year for the Dead. It was during 1970 that people began to record the concerts. They had done it previously, but now, it became a culture. Everyone who came to the concert brought with them a portable tape recorder, microphones and plenty of batteries so they wouldn't miss anything.

DEADHEADS

This early in their career, the fans were just fans, but as the phenomenon continues, by the late Seventies and early Eighties, the fans became known as "Deadheads." The term actually appeared in print the very first time on the liner notes of the second live album the band released, *Grateful Dead,* or as it also known as, *Skull and Roses,* which was released in November of 1971. In the liner notes of this album, the following appears:

"DEAD FREAKS UNITE: Who are you? Where are you? How are you? Send us your name and address and we'll keep you informed. Dead Heads, P.O. Box 1065, San Rafael, California 94901"

That is the first mention of the term in print.

1971 began with Mickey Hart in a bad way. He was really hurting over what his dad had done to the group. He would lapse into depression and talked of suicide. They tried to get him help, but he soon came to realize that he had to leave the band for a while, to get his head on straight. Now, they were five again and only one drum which meant they had to change the arrangements of their songs they played live. They said they had to play around the hole that Mickey left when he left the band.

To make matters worse, Pig was having difficulties. Pig had always been a strong personality. Now, he seemed withdrawn and tended to stay in the background more. He hadn't played that much in the last two albums and had only written one song in the last year or so. About this time, they took on a new lyricist, John Barlow, who mainly worked with Bob Weir. Bob had written a lot of songs with Robert Hunter, but friction had developed between them as Bob liked to improvise and Hunter wanted his work to be sung exactly like he had written it, so Bob joined up with Barlow and the two became a new writing team for the band.

Next, more death haunted the band. In the spring of 1971, both of Bob Weir's parents died within a week of each other. Now, Jerry's parents were both gone, Phil dad was gone, and Bob's parents were both gone. On September 17, 1971, Pigpen was taken to the hospital with a bleeding ulcer. It was a shock to everyone until they realized that Pig had been drinking since he was a teenager, and it was no surprise that it finally caught up to him.

KEITH AND DONNA GODCHAUX JOIN THE BAND

A replacement keyboard player had to be found and so they hired Keith Godchaux to play piano for them. Keith was a totally different personality than Pig, and it changed the entire dynamic of the band. He had never played a Grateful Dead song in his life but in the first rehearsal, he kept up just fine. It seemed like he had always been there. The guys were very impressed with Keith.

Keith Godchaux was born on July 19, 1948 in Seattle, Washington. When he was just a young boy, Keith and his family moved to Concord, California which is just outside of San Francisco. His father was a musician, so Keith got his talent legitimately. He took to music easily and was soon playing at all of the local clubs. He met his wife Donna in 1970 and soon, they were married. They got the job with the Grateful Dead by just walking up to Jerry and asking for it. Pig was ill at the time, and they needed a pianist and so they hired Keith and Donna.

A month or so later, Pig came and rejoined the band. Phil says he was shocked to see him. He seemed shrunken and frail. Pig had been through an ordeal, but he insisted he could play. In March of 1972, they decided they needed a female voice in the band and so they hired Keith Godchaux's wife, Donna to join the band as a vocalist. Now, the group was getting back to the crowd they were used to on stage.

Donna Godchaux was born Donna Jean Thatcher on August 22, 1947 in Muscle Shoals, Alabama. She started singing as early as age fifteen and actually sang on one of Elvis Presley's albums as a backup singer. She can be heard on Elvis' "Suspicious Minds" and she also sang on "When a Man Loves a Woman" recorded by Percy Sledge. In 1970, she moved to San Francisco, met and married Keith Godchaux, and became a member of the Grateful Dead. She stayed with the band until 1979 when she and Keith left the band to form their own group "Heart of Gold." Keith died in 1980 after only one performance of their new band, and Donna returned to her home in Alabama.

During 1972, the members of the band decided to do some solo work. Jerry Garcia released *Garcia*, a self-titled work on which Jerry played all the instruments. This came out in January of 1972, but the album did not chart. Most of the writing, however, was done by Jerry and his friend Robert Hunter. Bob Weir also released a solo album, *Ace*, in May of 1972. Even though this is said to be a solo album almost all of the Dead played on it, so it sounds much like a Grateful Dead album. Bob and his friend John Barlow did write most of the songs on the album. Mickey Hart also released an album in September of 1972 called *Rolling Thunder*. Mickey was not officially playing with the band when he released the album but most of the Dead joined him and played on the album. As far as I can tell, neither Bob's nor Mickey's albums charted.

THE DEATH OF PIGPEN

After a trip to Paris, Pigpen came down with hepatitis and had to leave the band temporarily to recover. He was frail and weak and everyone thought he would be back as soon as he got better. Unfortunately, it was not to be. On March 8, 1973, word came to the band that Pigpen had been found dead on the floor of his apartment in Corte Madera, California where he lived. He was 27 years old. He had played his last concert with the band on June 17, 1972 at the Hollywood Bowl in Los Angeles.

Pigpen died of a gastrointestinal hemorrhage caused by Crohn's Disease. Most people assume it was because of his drinking, but Crohn's is hereditary and his brother, Kevin, also died of the disease. He is buried at Alta Mesa Memorial Park in Palo Alto, California. Also buried there is Steve Jobs and Tennessee Ernie Ford and several other celebrities, so Pig has good company.

It was about this time that the band left Warner Brothers and established their own label, the *Grateful Dead* label (what else?) The first album for this new label was *Wake of the Flood*, which was also the first album without Pigpen. Using Keith Godchaux as their now full time keyboardist changed the sound of the band somewhat. Where Pigpen leaned toward blues, Keith was more a jazz artist and so the group had to get used to this new sound. Continuing their rise on the charts, *Wake of the Flood* reached number eighteen on the Billboard album charts which was higher than any previous album.

THE WALL OF SOUND

It was about this time that the famous "wall of sound" was perfected. When I think of the term "wall of sound", I think of Phil Spector and his girl groups from the early Sixties. It was said that the music in behind these girls was a wall of sound. The Dead took this idea to a whole new level. During a concert, the wall of sound was behind them on the stage. It was forty feet high and seventy feet wide and consisted of 600 speakers and 25,000 watts of power blasting out to the crowd. I don't know how the band kept their hearing with that kind of sound coming at them. There were six channels for the instruments and one channel for the vocals. The band now had ultimate control over how the music sounded to the audience.

Most Deadheads agreed the band had reached the pinnacle in their performances. Now, this system was expensive. They needed twice the crew to set up and tear down the set. That required more money and resulted in the band having to perform before more people, so they started playing larger venues in front of larger audiences. The Dead prided itself on being an intimate band. They liked to play small venues with a small audience. This new paradigm put a strain on the band and its members.

In 1974, they released their second album on the new label *From the Mars Hotel*, which contains three songs that were rarely ever played live. "Unbroken Chain," "Money Money," and "Pride of Cucamonga" were only played a few times (less than ten) and "Cucamonga" was never played live. The cover of the album depicts the Mars Hotel which is a flophouse in San Francisco. The graphic on the cover, which I can't read at all, is said to read "Ugly Rumours" if you turn it upside down and hold it up to a mirror. This was the inspiration of the British Prime Minister Tony Blair's band by the same name "Ugly Rumours."

After touring Europe in 1974, they decided to take some time off from the road. They only performed four times in 1975, and it showed. During 1975 – 1976, they released six albums under the new *Grateful Dead* label and the newly formed *Round Record* label which was created for their solo efforts. The first of these was *Tiger Rose* which was the second album Robert Hunter attempted as a solo artist. It did not sell well. Next was *Seastones* which was a solo effort by Phil Lesh collaborating with Ned Lagin. Released in April of 1975, the album is described as experimental space music. It probably didn't reach a very large audience. Jerry Garcia released *Old & In the Way* which was also the name of his band. It was an album of bluegrass music and actually did chart, peaking at number 99 on the Billboard album charts. It went on to become one of the best-selling bluegrass albums in history.

"BLUES FOR ALLAH"

The next studio album the Dead produced was *Blues for Allah* which was their bestselling and charting album to date, peaking at number twelve on the album charts. The title song was in honor of King Faisal of Saudi Arabia who had died in 1975. He was said to be a big fan of the Dead. There is some question as to how many times the title song was ever actually performed. Some say they did it in four or five concerts and then never performed it again.

Steal Your Face, a double album of live music was released on June 26 of 1976. Nobody was happy with the album. Jerry says they were just not working well together. Maybe they were still getting over the loss of Pigpen or maybe they had just been doing too much work separately. Phil called the album "abysmal," and "the worse album we ever made." The material was recorded back in 1974, when the band was going through a rough patch. They weren't getting along with one another. The tour that this album is taken from was actually called their "Farewell Tour." At that time, everyone was ready for a break.

They soon shut down Grateful Dead Records because of financial reasons. None of the albums they had produced were making any money. They then decided to sign with Arista. The group returned to full time touring in 1976 and by 1977 was going full speed. Deadheads consider 1977 to be a standout year for the band.

Although recorded in 1974 at the Winterland Ballroom in San Francisco, a concert movie was put together of their live performances and released in 1977. *The Grateful Dead Movie* was the closest some people would come to seeing the band live. Jerry Garcia directed the film. It's still available today on DVD in various formats. If you were lucky enough to catch it, the movie was shown in a one-night only fashion at select theaters on April 20 of 2011 and then repeated on

May 5. Write a letter to Fathom Events and maybe we'll get a chance to see it again.

The rest of the Seventies saw the release of two more albums. *Terrapin Station* was released in 1977 and was on Arista Records. It had a symphonic sound to it and wasn't as well received as previous albums. The fans wanted the basic Grateful Dead sound, not an orchestra, but it did reach number twenty eight on the album charts. The next album was *Shakedown Street* in late 1978. A highlight of this album, for me, is "Stagger Lee." Now, I immediately thought of the Lloyd Price song from 1959, but it turns out that "Stagger Lee" goes back to the turn of the century and was first recorded in 1923 by Fred Waring. It's about a murder that occurred in 1895 in St Louis, Missouri. Now the Dead's version of "Stagger Lee" is really the same story, but the words are different and the tune is definitely different and so writing credit for the song is given to Garcia/Hunter. If you haven't heard it, go find it on YouTube and give it a try. I liked it.

Shakedown Street continued the slide of Dead albums as it only peaked at number forty one.

THE EIGHTIES

In 1980, *Go To Heaven* was released. It would be their last "all-new material" album for eight years. It also was the first project that featured Brent Mydland on keyboards as both Donna and Keith Godchaux had left the band in 1979. The Godchaux couple found life on the road just too difficult. They had a child at home that they never saw, and it was destroying their marriage so after a meeting with the band, they decided to call it quits. They hired Brent Mydland to take Keith's place. It was only a year later that Keith was killed in an automobile accident.

The album, *Go To Heaven*, did a little better than previous efforts, peaking at number twenty three on the album charts. The next year, 1981, they released two live albums which were compilations of clips from concerts done in various places. *Reckoning* and *Dead Set* were both released that year. They were meant to complement each other. *Reckoning* (originally called *Dead Reckoning*) was essentially an acoustic album and was released April 1. *Dead Set* is the electric cousin to *Reckoning* and wasn't released until August. All of the music was recorded at the same concerts, and they originally intended to release it as a double album and then decided to release two different albums instead.

The band had been asked to do benefit concerts at various times and sometimes they were able to do so, but a large number of times, it just didn't fit into their schedule. So, in 1983, they created the Rex Foundation which was a non-profit organization designed specially to give money to causes that the band deemed worthy. It was named after Rex Jackson, a road manager that had been killed in an automobile accident back in 1976. Between 1984 and 1995, the foundation gave away more than $7 million to over 1000 causes that they believed in.

The Eighties went by in a blur. They toured. Then they toured some more. Phil met his soul mate, Jill (in Phil's autobiography he says her name is Jillspeth Winifred) and they were married. They still are. Drugs were a pretty big part of the band's life during the Eighties. Jerry Garcia had gotten into heroin, and they all did cocaine at regular times. It was about this time that the guys noticed that the faces in the front row were familiar. The fans were traveling with the band and, thus, the term Deadhead, really came into its own.

The Deadheads were taping every concert, and they were open about it. Microphones started appearing in the crowd. It got so bad that the guys created a special place at each concert called "the tapers" zone where the people who were taping could go. It costs money to travel around and follow a band, especially since the Deadheads weren't working, at least not while they were on the road, so the fans started setting up vendor stands around the perimeter of the concert where they sold food, drinks, posters, tie-dye tee-shirts, and other assorted Grateful Dead paraphernalia. The area became known as "Shakedown Street," but I'm not sure if it's named after the album or the album is named after the phenomenon. The Deadheads became a culture all their own. You'd think this would annoy the guys in the band, but they loved it. It represented everything they stood for as a band.

JERRY GOES THROUGH A ROUGH PATCH

Jerry's health was deteriorating rapidly. The years of drug use were catching up to him. He started putting on weight and during brief intervals between songs, he could be seen resting his chin on the microphone. The band was concerned and decided an intervention was appropriate. They sat him down and talked to him, and he agreed to enter a drug rehabilitation program. They told him his choices were get clean or leave the band, although I can't imagine them throwing him out of the band. This was January of 1985.

Jerry did believe they might fire him, and he agreed to the rehabilitation. Before he could start, however, the police busted him for drug possession. The judge said he wouldn't go to jail if he attended the drug "diversion" program, which he did. By 1986, Jerry was clean.

It might have been a too little, too late kind of situation. In July of 1986 he lapsed into a diabetic coma and had to be hospitalized. He was in a coma for five days. When he got out of the hospital, he literally had to learn how to play the guitar all over again along with a number of other basic skills, but it didn't take long for him to get back on his feet and by the end of 1986; he was back with the band, playing as good as he ever did.

It was during all of this that Jerry was living with a woman named Manasha Matheson or at least he spent a lot of time in her company. The two had a daughter together in late 1987 named Keelin. Keelin was Jerry's fourth and final child. I don't believe he and Manasha ever married.

"TOUCH OF GRAY"

As a sort of come-back album, in early 1987, the band recorded and released *In the Dark* which would become the highest selling album of their career. It's called that because during the recording of the album, someone turned off all the lights in the studio. I think it was intended as a joke and everybody laughed and just kept on playing. It was their first album since 1980 and the fans were grateful (no pun intended) that they were back. The album would chart higher than any album up to this point and, as it turns out, any album after this. It reached number six on the Billboard Album Charts.

The standout song from *In the Dark* has to be "Touch of Gray" which is their only single to crack the Top 40, peaking at number nine on the Billboard Hot 100 singles chart. It also hit number one on the Mainstream Rock Charts, one of the lesser known Billboard charts. This is the Dead's only song to hit both charts. It was also the first song they did a video for. If you have a chance, go watch it on YouTube. The band is live people one minute and skeletons the next. It's a great song, one of my favorites.

The lyrics in "Touch of Gray" which Jerry sings: "I will survive" is a direct reference to the coma from back in 1986. It had taken him several months to get back to the band after the incident, but he was still around and he will survive.

Trouble seemed to follow the band, however. In 1989, the police finally realized that if they watched the Grateful Dead concerts carefully, they would see drug use. At two Pittsburg, Pennsylvania concerts in April, there were fifty-five arrests for drug possession. This wasn't the band being arrested, but the fans in the crowd. That same month, seventy fans were arrested in Irving, California for drug possession and vandalism. In October, an over exuberant fan somehow fell and broke his neck and died. No one was ever arrested for it, so it was ruled an accident. Finally, in December, a fan who had been arrested for possession, died in police custody in Los Angeles. This had been a tough year, and it prompted the band to issue a warning to the fans (Deadheads) to act and use responsibly.

In 1989, they released two albums. The first was a live album *Dylan and the Dead* which was a collaborative album with Bob Dylan and the band. It was poorly received but did make it to number thirty seven on the album charts. The second was *Built to Last* which came out on Halloween, 1989. *Built to Last* would turn out to be the last studio album released by the Grateful Dead under that name. It did fairly well, reaching number twenty seven on the charts.

About a year later Brent Mydland died of an overdose of a drug called speedball. This is a form of cocaine which is injected. I find that particularly disturbing since the band had gone to so much trouble just five years earlier to get Jerry free of drugs. Ironically, Brent was scheduled to enter rehab the next day and had spent "one last night" with his favorite drugs as kind of a going away party. He overdosed and that was the end. Brent had been their keyboardist for eleven years, longer than any other in the band's history. It had a profound effect on them. It affected Jerry probably the most. He wondered if the band would ever be the same again.

The last album Brent played on was released in September of 1990. *Without a Net* was another live album. They replaced Brent with two keyboardists: Vince Welnick and Bruce Hornsby. Hornsby had already had a successful career of his own and even a number one hit in 1986 with "The Way It Is." He would play off and on for the band during 1990 and 1991. When he saw that Vince could handle the job on his own, he left the band and went back to his own career. One big problem was that Jerry was using again. He was getting older and was tired and it showed on stage. The band considered another intervention, and one night after a concert in Denver, they confronted him again. The meeting did not go well, but Jerry knew he had to do something, so he sat down with Phil and told him he would clean himself up this time. He was taking meth and so started attending a clinic for methadone users. After their tour in 1992, Jerry became very sick. The drug use was really catching up to him. He hired a personal doctor to attend to him, and the entire fall tour of 1992 was cancelled. Over the next year or two, Jerry's health continued to decline. He did stop smoking, and he started to lose weight which was a good sign. Since his coma in 1986, he had become a vegetarian and that also helped him somewhat.

THE END OF THE GRATEFUL DEAD

By the beginning of 1995, Jerry's health had continued to deteriorate. He was having trouble both physically and mentally. He would try to play during a concert and forget what song they were playing. He started using narcotics again just to ease the pain that he was feeling.

In July of 1995, he checked himself into the Betty Ford Clinic and was encouraged by the help he got there but for some reason only stayed two weeks and then left. He then tried Serenity Knolls treatment center located in Forest Knolls, California. On the morning of August 9, 1995, an attendant found Jerry lying on the floor of his room, dead of an apparent heart attack. They tried to revive him, but at 4:23 a.m., pronounced him dead. He was fifty three years old.

The last Grateful Dead concert was held on July 9, 1995 at Soldier Field in Chicago, Illinois. This was the last time the band performed together before Jerry left them.

It sent a shock wave throughout the musical world and especially the members of the band. Phil would say, "I was struck numb. I had lost my oldest, surviving friend, my brother." Two days later, on August 11, services were held at St. Stephen's Episcopal Church in Belvedere, California. The entire band was there, including some former members like Bruce Hornsby and Bob Dylan. In an odd turn of events, Jerry's widow, Deborah, refused to let either of his first two wives attend the funeral.

In response to the death, Deadheads from everywhere were congregating at Polo Fields in Golden Gate Park in San Francisco. A stage was set up along with a 30 foot picture of Jerry Garcia and some of the band came and played for the crowd. There were thousands of flowers and other mementos placed around the outside of the field to honor Jerry. The crowd reached over 25,000 people, all there to pay their respects to a great man and a great musician. Here was a man who touched everyone he met and everyone who had ever heard him play.

Jerry was cremated, so there is no grave to visit. In April of 1996, Bob Weir and his wife, Deborah took some of the ashes to India and spread them in the Ganges River. Later that month, they took the rest of his ashes and deposited them in the Pacific Ocean right near the Golden Gate Bridge.

Now, what to do? Jerry was gone. The group got together to discuss their options. Bill had already moved to Hawaii and was on speaker phone. The first thing he said was, "I don't want to tour anymore." Everyone in the room breathed a sigh of relief. He had said what everyone was thinking. The Grateful Dead were, for all intents and purposes, well, dead. It would be several years before the remaining members of the band would play together again.

AFTER THE DEAD

The members went their own ways and soon started other bands. One notable group was "The Other Ones" which consisted of mainly ex-Dead people. It featured Bob Weir, Phil Lesh, Mickey Hart, and their old friend Bruce Hornsby. People came and went over the next few years. Phil left, Bill Kreutzmann joined, Phil rejoined, and Bruce Hornby left. Finally, in 2003, they changed the name to the Dead. The Dead was really the Grateful Dead without Jerry, and they performed together off and on until 2009. The tour that year was their last to date, but, who knows they could come back and do another one.

Phil Lesh, after a serious bout with liver disease that required a liver transplant, formed "Phil Lesh and Friends." He and his wife, Jill spend time running a charity organization called the "Unbroken Chain Foundation" which attempts to further the work done by the Grateful Dead. The goal is to hold concerts and other events which will bring in money for worthwhile nonprofit organizations. Phil and Jill have two children, Grahame and Brian, who are now old enough to play with their father in the band.

Soon after Jerry's death, Bob Weir formed a new band called "Ratdog Revue" which was quickly shortened to just "Ratdog." While performing in the other incarnations of the remaining Dead members, Weir performed some 800 concerts with "Ratdog." They have performed as recently as March of 2013.

One thing that impresses me about the members of the Grateful Dead is their belief in helping others. The band did a great deal of humanitarian work while they were together and the individual members continued that after the band ceased to exist. Bob Weir is on the board of directors for the Rex Foundation which I talked about earlier. He is active in Rainforest Action network which is an environmental organization. He is also on the board of directors of "Little Kids Rock," an organization designed to help kids get musical instruments free of charge in areas where they can't do it on their own.

Bill Kreutzmann formed another band right away, called "Backbone." It consisted of three people, including Bill, and they released one album in 1998 before Bill went on to join "The Other Ones." In between the Dead collaborations, Bill worked with a band called "Trichromes" which included Journey guitarist Neal Schon. They released one album. In 2006, he got together with his old friend Mickey Hart and a couple other people to form the "Rhythm Devils." They performed at least through 2008, performing new songs written by the Grateful Dead lyricist, Robert Hunter. As recently as 2010, he formed a new band called "7 Walkers," which some think is named after a Grateful Dead song. They also have released an album.

In 1995, Bill produced a video called *Ocean Space* which is a documentary about the ocean and its ecosystem. Another member of the Dead trying to make the world a better place. Bill is also a visual artist and has produced many limited editions of his work. They are available through Walker Street Gallery in Denver, Colorado. I checked out a few of the prints that are available for sale (ranging from $650.00 and up) and they are very cool. I wish I could afford one; I would have it hanging on my wall right now.

One last band to talk about is "Furthur," named after the bus that Ken Kesey used to drive people around in the Sixties during the "Acid Test" years. Formed by Phil Lesh and Bob Weir and three other guys in 2009, Furthur plays mainly music from the Grateful Dead catalog and are still performing to this day. This band, right now, is probably as close as you'll come to hearing the Dead in a live setting. If they come near you and you're a fan, make sure you see them play.

The Grateful Dead lives on. I believe the influence that was felt as a result of the Grateful Music will be felt for years and decades to come.

Long after we are all gone, Grateful Dead music will still be heard somewhere on this planet. Shortly after Jerry's death, their archivist, Dick Latvala, started issuing the many, many concerts that had been recorded over the years. Called *Dick's Picks*, there are now 36 volumes released between 1993 and 2005. I gave some thought to listing them in the discography, but it is a long list and the real fan can find them on the internet.

After Dick's Picks stopped, they next released a series of albums called *Road Trips*. This started in 2007 and continued to about 2011. It consists of seventeen compilations of other concerts that hadn't been released anywhere else.

Dick Latvala died in 1999 and taking his place was David Lemieux, who became the archivist for the band. Between February, 2012 and the present time (September, 2013), there have been seven *Dave's Picks* released which are the same format as *Dick's Picks*. I have no reason to believe that they will not continue to be released, and you will have an opportunity to pick up new music from the Grateful Dead.

During the 30 years that the Dead played from 1965 until 1995, when Jerry died, they performed in some 2300 shows, and I suspect there is someone in the world that has a recording of all of them. The band contained thirteen different people at different times, as personnel changed and people came and went, but there were only four who played in every one of those 2300 concerts. They were, of course, Jerry Garcia, Phil Lesh, Bill Kreutzmann, and Bob Weir. I suspect if Pigpen hadn't passed away when he did, he would have been with them until the end as well.

The Dead never performed a concert with a play sheet. Most bands know ahead of time exactly what they are going to play and in what order before they even step onto the stage. But the Dead did not do that. They played according to what moved them at the time. They would kick off the concert with some number that they thought of right at the moment and then that would lead into another song and likely, at the end of one song, one of the members would yell out the name of what he would like to play next and they would launch into that. I think this is what made the concerts so unique to the fans. You never knew what you would hear when you went to a Grateful Dead concert. They were all different and they were all unique and, I think, that is why people liked to collect each and every one.

Phil Lesh, in his autobiography *Searching for the Sound – My Life with the Grateful Dead* said this in his closing remarks, *"Like family members who still celebrate with one another after the patriarch of the family has passed on, my brothers and I play on, and I always feel Jerry's presence at our shows. No one can be replaced in the hearts of those who love them, but I still feel the necessity to play — for those who come to dance and those who hope to find magic, communing together with friends and family."* I have read this entire book and recommend it for anyone who wants a more in-depth look at the Grateful Dead.

"They'll follow me down any dark alley," Garcia noted in 1987. *"Sometimes there's light at the end of the tunnel, and sometimes there's a dark hole. The point is: you don't get adventure in music unless you're willing to take chances."*

LEGACY OF THE GRATEFUL DEAD

All five members of the original band were inducted into the Rock and Roll Hall of Fame in 1994. Also included were members who had played with the band temporarily at different times. The following were inducted: Tom Constanten, Jerry Garcia, Donna Jean Godchaux, Keith Godchaux, Mickey Hart, Robert Hunter, Bill Kreutzmann, Phil Lesh, Ron McKernan, Brent Mydland, Bob Weir, and Vince Welnick

Jerry appeared briefly in the movie *Close Encounters of the Third Kind* in 1977 as an extra in a crowd scene which was shot in India.

In 1987 ice cream manufacturers Ben & Jerry created a flavor just to honor Jerry Garcia called *Cherry Garcia.*

Jerry Garcia is ranked by *Rolling Stone Magazine* as number thirteen on their list of the 100 Greatest Guitar Players of All Time.

The band itself is ranked number 57 of *Rolling Stone Magazine's* list of the Greatest Artists of All Time.

Their concert at Barton Hall on the Cornell University campus in 1977 has been added to the Library of Congress's Recording Registry.

The Grateful Dead have sold more than 35 Million albums in their career. How many were recorded and sold under the table is anybody's guess.

The Grateful Dead performed about 2300 concerts in the 30 years they were performing. Of these, it's estimated that almost 2200 of them were taped and most of these are available somewhere online.

On April 28, 2008, a press conference was held by Bob Weir and Mickey Hart, and they announced that the McHenry Library on the University of California, Santa Cruz campus would be the permanent holding place of the entire archival history of the Grateful Dead from 1965 until the present.

At the 2007 Grammy Awards, held on February 10, the band was presented with the Lifetime Achievement Award. It was accepted by Mickey Hart and Bill Kreutzmann.

AFTERWORD

The career of the Grateful Dead can be viewed in several stages. During the last half of the Sixties, they were a psychedelic rock band and everyone related them to the San Francisco scene of the day. In the Seventies, they tended more toward the roots of folk and rock music and were noted for their long jams on stage. It was during this period that they picked up the Deadheads. In the Eighties and Nineties, they were known for their tours and in the early Nineties, they were the highest grossing band on the road.

The group varied in number over the years. Starting with five members, they, at times, had as many as seven. Four members of the Grateful Dead (not counting Jerry Garcia) all died young and what is even stranger all four were keyboardists, Ron "Pigpen" McKernan (1973), Keith Godchaux (1980), Brent Mydland (1990), and Vince Welnick (2006).

Mickey Hart once said, *"We are in the transportation business. We move minds"* and that sums up the Grateful Dead in one sentence. If you are a fan, then you understand and know what I mean. If you're not, then get on YouTube or go buy an album and become a fan. You won't be sorry.

You can contact me at www.number1project.com where I occasionally blog about things that interest me in the music world (mostly, the twentieth century). Go find it and read it and leave me a comment. I also have a Facebook fan page called "Legends of Rock & Roll". "Like" me and comment there, too. If you love the music as much as I do, you'll enjoy the trip. Thanks for reading.

I hope you have enjoyed this book as much as I have enjoyed writing it for you.

If you have liked what you read, will you please do me a favor and leave a review of "The Grateful Dead". Thank you.

ABOUT THE AUTHOR

James Hoag has always been a big fan of Rock & Roll. Most people graduate from high school and then proceed to "grow up" and go on to more adult types of music. James got stuck at about age 18 and has been an avid fan of popular music ever since. His favorite music is from the Fifties, the origin of Rock & Roll and which was the era in which James grew up. But he likes almost all types of popular music including country music.

After working his entire life as a computer programmer, he is now retired and he decided to share his love of the music and of the performers by writing books that discuss the life and music of the various people who have meant so much to him over the years.

He calls each book a "love letter" to the stars that have enriched our lives so much. These people are truly Legends.

SELECTED DISCOGRAPHY

Albums

It is almost impossible to list all of the albums that were recorded by the Grateful Dead. In the Eighties and Nineties, there was a thriving underground business of recording and selling every concert that they performed. I list here, the mainstream albums which were legal and available at some point.

1967 - The Grateful Dead

1968 - Anthem of the Sun

1969 - Aoxomoxoa

1969 - Live/Dead

1970 - Workingman's Dead

1970 - American Beauty

1971 - Grateful Dead (also known as Skull and Roses)

1972 - Europe '72

1973 - History of the Grateful Dead, Volume One (Bear's Choice)

1973 - Wake of the Flood

1974 - From the Mars Hotel

1975 - Blues for Allah

1976 - Steal Your Face

1977 - Terrapin Station

1978 - Shakedown Street

1980 - Go to Heaven

1981 - Reckoning

1981 - Dead Set

1987 - In the Dark

1989 - Dylan & the Dead

1989 - Built to Last

1990 - Without a Net

Compilation Albums

1974 - Skeletons from the Closet: The Best of Grateful Dead

1977 - What a Long Strange Trip It's Been

1996 - The Arista Years

1997 - Selections From the Arista Years

2003 - The Very Best of the Grateful Dead

2011 - Flashback with the Grateful Dead

Box Sets

1987 - Dead Zone: The Grateful Dead CD Collection (1977-1987)

2001 - The Golden Road (1965–1973)

2004 - Beyond Description (1973-1989)

2010 - The Warner Bros. Studio Albums

2012 - All the Years Combine: The DVD Collection

Retrospective Live Albums (Traditional releases)

1991 - One From the Vault

1991 - Infrared Roses

1992 - Two from the Vault

1994 - Grayfolded

1995 - Hundred Year Hall

1996 - Dozin' at the Knick

1997 - Fallout from the Phil Zone

1997 - Terrapin Station (Limited Edition)

1997 - Live at the Fillmore East 2-11-69

1999 - So Many Roads (1965–1995)

1999 - So Many Roads (1965-1995) Sampler

2000 - View from the Vault, Volume One

2000 - Ladies and Gentlemen... the Grateful Dead

2001 - View from the Vault, Volume Two

2001 - Nightfall of Diamonds

2002 - Postcards of the Hanging

2002 - Steppin' Out with the Grateful Dead: England '72

2002 - View from the Vault, Volume Three

2002 - Go to Nassau

2003 - Birth of the Dead

2003 - View from the Vault, Volume Four

2003 - The Closing of Winterland

2004 - Rockin' the Rhein with the Grateful Dead

2005 - The Grateful Dead Movie Soundtrack

2005 - Rare Cuts and Oddities 1966

2005 - Truckin' Up to Buffalo

2005 - Fillmore West 1969: The Complete Recordings

2005 - Fillmore West 1969

2007 - Live at the Cow Palace

2007 - Three from the Vault

2008 - Winterland 1973: The Complete Recordings

2008 - Rocking the Cradle: Egypt 1978

2009 - To Terrapin: Hartford '77

2009 - Winterland June 1977: The Complete Recordings

2010 - Crimson White & Indigo

2010 - Formerly the Warlocks

2011 - Europe '72: The Complete Recordings

2011 - Europe '72 Volume 2

2012 - Spring 1990

2012 - Spring 1990: So Glad You Made It

2012 - Winterland: May 30th 1971

2013 - May 1977

Dick's Picks

There were 36 Volumes of Dick's Picks released between 1993 and 2005

Road Trips

There were seventeen Road Trips albums released between 2007 and 2011

Dave's Picks

So far, there have been seven Dave's Picks released up to the present time. (2013)

Singles

1966 - "Stealin'"

1967 - "The Golden Road (To Unlimited Devotion)"

1967 - "Viola Lee Blues"

1968 - "Dark Star"

1969 - "Dupree's Diamond Blues"

1969 - "China Cat Sunflower"

1970 - "Uncle John's Band"

1970 - "Casey Jones"

1970 - "Truckin'"

1972 - "One More Saturday Night"

1972 - "Johnny B. Goode"

1973 - "Sugar Magnolia"

1973 - "Let Me Sing Your Blues Away"

1973 - "Eyes Of The World"

1974 - "U.S. Blues"

1975 - "The Music Never Stopped"

1975 - "Franklin's Tower"

1977 - "Dancin' in the Streets"

1977 - "Passenger"

1978 - "Good Lovin'"

1979 - "Shakedown Street"

1980 - "Alabama Getaway"

1980 - "Don't Ease Me In"

1981 - "Dire Wolf"

1987 - "Touch of Grey"

1987 - "Hell In A Bucket"

1987 - "Throwing Stones"

1989 - "Foolish Heart"